9[0] THOUGHTS

FOR SMALLER CHURCH YOUTH WORKERS

DOING MORE WITH LESS

BY STEPHANIE CARO

99 Thoughts for Smaller Church Youth Workers
Doing More With Less

Credits
Author: Stephanie Caro
Executive Developer: Nadim Najm
Chief Creative Officer: Joani Schultz
Copy Editor: Rob Cunningham
Cover Art and Production: Natalie Johnson and Veronica Lucas
Production Manager: DeAnne Lear

ISBN 978-0-7644-6606-9

10 9 8 7 6 5 4 3 2 1   20 19 18 17 16 15 14 13 12 11

Printed in the United States of America.

dedication

This book is dedicated to a delightful group of youth ministry friends, the SYMC Inside Track Team. You bring me joy and laughter on a daily basis and inspire me to keep doing this youth ministry thing. You have captured a permanent place in my heart.

contents

Introduction 1

The Big Advantage 3

Running With the Big Dogs. 13

The Vortex of Volunteers 25

It's a Balancing Act. 39

The Particulars on Parents 51

The Oddities of a Smaller Group. 61

Navigating Your Church's Channels 73

Doing More Ministry With Less Money 83

A Few of My Favorite Things. 93

Four Things I Wish Someone 103
Told Me Earlier

introduction

Hey, my youth ministry friends!

If you're reading this book, the intertwining of our lives has begun. If you're serving in a smaller church youth ministry, the weaving continues. I've served in large and small youth ministries. Both are wonderful and both drive me nuts! One thing that remains constant: Students need the love of Jesus and Jesus-followers. That's where we both come on to the scene.

From my heart to yours, I really want this book to be a conversation between you and me. I've invited several smaller church youth workers to join the book's conversation by adding their thoughts into each chapter. We're all in this together with one goal, right? Sharing the love of God with students (and the adults who work with them) in our ministries. From the bottom of my heart, I L.O.V.E. how so many of us have connected through the Simply Youth Ministry blog, smallchurchyouthministry.com, Facebook® (friend me!), and Twitter®.

If you're looking for deep, theological brainiac-ness, then go read something else. Youth workers in smaller churches are often volunteer or part-time/bi-vocational. We're busy people who need to read what's quick and practical. In the pages to follow, you'll find 99 extended thoughts divided into 10 topic buckets we all may face while living out life with students. Each bucket of thoughts will focus through the lens of a smaller church setting. Sometimes the struggles aren't different from what youth workers face in medium-sized or larger church youth ministries. But a lot of times, we face a special brand of monster.

To borrow from God's Word, here's how I see our partnered journey as youth workers trying to hang on tight while praying to make a Jesus-impact:

By yourself you're unprotected. With a friend you can face the worst. Can you round up a third? A three-stranded rope isn't easily snapped (Ecclesiastes 4:12 The Message).

See ya at the end of the book…unless you'd like to chat along the way on our blog.

Grab some coffee and stop by smallchurchyouthministry.com.

Stephanie

Stephanie

the big advantage

THOUGHT #1

I want to know every student's name

Every summer, I spend several weeks back in "big youth group" world as an emcee for Group Workcamps. Oh the cacophony of noise! The sounds of more than 400 students living under one roof for a week is a special joy all its own. It's not for wimps or the faint of heart. There is this constant noise like the hum of a plague of nighttime bugs. You learn a certain type of selective deafness—what to ignore and when to pay attention to a certain squeal that spells trouble. And if it becomes too quiet? Run for your flashlight and start searching the halls 'cuz there's trouble in River City, my friend!

I love it! I love mission trips, making new friends, the sense of God incarnate, spending time with youth, and the dumb late-night knock-knock jokes. But here's what I *hate* about this annual experience: The week will go by and I'll see a student that looks totally unfamiliar to me. With 400-plus campers, I learn 100 names at best. Although I still feel the sense of God's family, I mourn the missed opportunity of showing that student—and all the ones I don't get to know well—I really do care about who they are.

Aren't we lucky to serve in smaller settings? We can learn each student's name, favorite food, birthday, likes, dislikes, movie preference, and so on. So here's your homework: Picture all the teenagers that come to your youth program. Can you name 10 particulars about each person? Work on that...aren't we lucky? We get to do this!

THOUGHT #2

It's not like turning the Titanic around

Big boats require a lot of effort to turn around. They can't do it easily and often need the help of many other small boats to get in and out of port. In their bigness, they can hold huge numbers of people, but if a midcourse correction is needed, a lot of folks have to sign off after a lot of communication.

Not with a small boat. It's just you, the water, and sails or an engine. Changing your mind or changing directions leaves a small wake. Though it's still wise to let someone know you've modified your course, it's a simpler, easier process.

The same with your youth ministry. You can change course more quickly because you don't have to jump through as many hoops. Don't misunderstand me: I'm not advocating skipping any proper approval process in your church's administration. It's just simpler and easier in a smaller setting. For example: You get word at the last minute that a student broke his leg. With a smaller group, you can spread the word to everyone that you're taking your weekly youth group meeting on the road to deliver cheer to their injured peer—perhaps serenading him outside his window with a big candy gram. Being small gives your ministry agility and flexibility.

THOUGHT #3

Even the little things make your students happy

Maybe I'm wrong, but in smaller churches and smaller youth ministries, I think teenagers are happier with whatever comes their way. I've served in big settings where it felt like demands were higher and there was less room for failure. Teenagers in smaller churches often excel at appreciating what the church does together, and they find ways to be satiated by enjoying one another's company.

I'm not saying it's OK to give your students less than your very best. I'm saying that smaller groups of teenagers seem to be happier with each other—it doesn't take the big woo-hoo that's often required and expected in bigger youth ministries. One of the best nights my students and I ever had was when I taught them how to play the card game

Spoons at a Christmas week lock-in. You'd have thought it was the newest thing around, and we had *so much* fun!

Maybe it's all in the presentation. If it looks like you just threw things together for your students, it'll come across that way and they'll respond accordingly. But with a little thought, even a simple Spoons championship can feel like a meaningful, well-executed event. Not only did I teach them the game, but I also gave each student a deck of Santa cards and a set of spoons. They must have liked it—because they got in trouble for playing the game during church the next Sunday.

THOUGHT #4

You *can* visit *every* single one of them!

One of the cardinal rules of "how to be even just a mediocre youth worker" is visiting students at their games, matches, concerts, plays, art shows, dance recitals, spelling bees, work-release programs, and so on. If you don't make this a practice and priority, you probably should look for another ministry role because youth ministry isn't your thing.

Teenagers are craving to have you come watch them do what they do. No need to gush or make a huge deal of it. Your quiet presence watching them do their thing will be noticed. And they won't forget it. It communicates that you care about them personally, and that's way up there on a youth worker's job description.

Since you don't have a huge number of students to work into your schedule, you have the opportunity to excel at this. Some savvy tips? Make sure the student and his or her parents see you there. Introduce yourself to the coach, director, principal, or whoever is leading the program or event. Keep track of which students you've visited and when; that way, you don't miss anyone and you play fair. A great follow-up is to send a card the day after your visit or the event. This creates a double blessing for the teenager. And if you ever get a chance to chaperone at a school event, take it! You'll probably see a bunch of your students all at once.

THOUGHT #5

One (hyphenated) word: Multi-generational!

Many smaller church youth groups find themselves an integral part of church-wide events; their attendance or absence is always noted. In fact, spaghetti suppers and movie nights are fantastic ways for your youth to serve the church. One struggle at many larger churches is a "silo" mentality—ministries that are self-contained unto themselves. (Think of the corn, wheat, and black-eyed peas silos on a farm; they're self-contained and never mix.)

I've heard one story after another about how the total (smaller) church comes together for such things as VBS, yard sales, and potlucks. My church couldn't survive without our students' ability to come and turn the pumpkins in our annual pumpkin patch. The urban myth that says teenagers don't want to spend time with the total church is just that: a myth.

Here's an example from my friend Karen Johns, who has spent nine years serving in youth ministry at a church in Kettering, Ohio:

"An interesting part of Sugar Creek Presbyterian is the mixture of generations in its programming. A major strength is the way the youth and adults work together. The youth have a chance to build true multi-generational relationships: adults serving as confirmation mentors; a sixth-grader and 90-year-old singing in the same choir; youth taking initiative in creating meaningful church-wide mission experiences; people of all ages leading worship as liturgists; talent shows where generations of families perform together...the list goes on! Our youth are a part of the living church; they are supported, nurtured, and loved as they learn their role in the world."

THOUGHT #6

Yeah, we have less money, but it's easier to get more

I remember the ancient days in the 1990s (I was 12) when my youth budget was close to $50K, and that didn't include

my salary or our fundraising. I had no idea how good I had it. It paid for my cell phone (yes we had cell phones—really big ones!), all the book resources I needed, training events for me and 25 of my volunteers, two interns, all volunteer expenses, and so on. If we needed it, we had the money for it.

These days, I don't even know what to say about that enormous budget. I can submit whatever budget I want to my boss, but I always hear these words: "You know we just don't have the money right now." You've probably heard those words, too!

Weird dynamic, though. When I had the larger youth ministry and budgets, I handled a lot more paperwork and witnessed a lot less on-the-spot generosity. Maybe there was an attitude rooted in this thought: "Isn't that what their budget is for?" In a smaller church, everyone knows there's no money for the youth group, so it's easier to just ask for what we need, like money for camp. We get it! Sure we do fundraisers—but we also ask and invite people to sponsor individual students and it just happens. God is good!

THOUGHT #7

Heaven in the real world

The world of youth ministry in smaller churches is populated with *way* more volunteer or part-time lead youth workers than full-time youth pastors. Most lead youth workers also work another job. Here's a glass-mostly-full way to look at this. Being on staff full time at a church can be great—but it can also be a small, narrow world. In my experience, having another job or being out in the world has made me better in my ministry. We're standing on the highways and byways of our culture and our communities with an opportunity to be Jesus in less sheltered circumstances. I like the advantage a "real world" job gives me to meet and reach people who might not come through the doors of my church.

THOUGHT #8

There's a weird freedom

When I had the big youth ministry jobs, I faced a lot of pressure to succeed. The big budget and salary are accompanied by a certain entitlement from church members—a sense of ownership that can roll outside of healthy boundaries. With a big salary came the external pressure of church members with big expectations and demands. With a big salary came the internal pressure of being all things youth ministry to all parties concerned.

Not now. In a smaller church, I feel a lack of performance pressure. There's not as much to lose. Strangely enough, it gives me freedom to be less insecure, which makes me stronger and bolder in service. Decisions aren't based on the fear of losing my job and not being able to support my family—they're based on determining what matters most: loving God and loving students. When you make lousy money—or no pay at all—in youth ministry, you're *really* not doing it for the money. Just a fun fact of youth ministry life.

THOUGHT #9

More than a manager

I'm gonna let my friend Darren Sutton, from Corpus Christi, Texas, share his thought on this:

*"I love being able to be more than a manager. When I served in a huge church, I spent most of my time administering and developing adult leadership (which I love)...but it's not the only thing I love. I like knowing most of my kids and their families well. I like being able to be 'interrupted' by kids and not find myself three weeks behind. I like knowing **lots** of adults in the church who have the potential to serve in the student ministry."*

THOUGHT #10

The family factor

Later on we'll chat about the challenges of multi-age levels in a smaller setting, but here's a positive spin from my friend Kim Dearborn from Grace United Methodist Church in Grove City, Pennsylvania:

"My students have the opportunity to attend the megachurch youth group down the street yet continue to attend our youth group because they say it feels like a family. Most of my older students are very protective and willing to mentor the younger students. I love knowing that my students take what we learn and hold each other accountable because they are all comfortable with one another. I feel that a smaller youth group enables you to know each student in a more personal way and you can be much more involved in their daily lives."

Smaller youth groups seem to embrace the mixing of age-stages. I think they instinctively understand the need for critical mass for "group events," which seems to gel around five people (though less than five can feel good for small group study).

running with the big dogs

Guests don't have the secret password for St. Small

We've covered the advantages of being a more intimately sized church. But we also must avoid certain pitfalls, and one of those pitfalls is how your guests navigate their initial visits to your church. Read what my friend John Mulholland at Eastview Christian Church in Cedar Rapids, Iowa, has to say:

"On July 4th of this year, we had a new family attend our worship service, a husband and wife with three children. During the service, the announcement came that 'Our children are now dismissed for their own worship service.' I watched as this family looked around for any cue as to which age group this was for: their youngest, a third-grader? Their older boys? Only when they saw the other younger children get up and walk toward the back did the mother get up with the girl and walk her out. This could have easily been resolved with an additional statement that 'Children's

13

worship is for kids pre-K through grade 5.' We've got to stop assuming that people know what we're thinking!"

In general, larger churches have figured out that not everyone knows what's going on; they've responded with unambiguous bulletins, simple-yet-complete signage, and platform conversation directed toward guests. Leaders at smaller churches tend to assume too much; this could explain why smaller churches often struggle to retain guests. New people don't want to feel like they need a secret code to understand how a church or youth ministry operates.

THOUGHT #12

Politics schmolitics

The politics of youth ministry in a smaller church are— hmmmm, shall we say "different" than a bigger church. "Politics? In our church?" Oh yeah, that's exactly what I'm saying. If you don't see any church politics going on in your church, it's because you started in youth ministry two hours ago.

Church politics exist in every church. I conduct youth and children's ministry assessments in all types and sizes of churches, and measuring the health factor of the political dynamics is always a part of the assessment process. You'd think the church would be the last place anyone would have to walk on the egg shells of who's in what leadership position, who donated what, and who's related to whom— but you'd be naïve for sticking to that train of thought.

My answer to this? Be savvy but not suspicious. Be shrewd but not shrill. Be wise but not a wisenheimer.

Smaller churches can't do everything— and that's OK

God has called some churches to be mega and some to be mini. Each one has its place, purpose, and plan. If you're part of a smaller church or a smaller youth ministry, you have limited time, people, and financial resources to go around, so how do you focus on what matters most? Invest in the youth and children's ministry.

Yes, I know what people say next. "But what about the women's group, men's ministry, small groups, prison outreach, dance team, soup kitchen, outreach to mimes, and street clowning? Shouldn't we fund those, too?" Yes, eventually—if God has called your church to that ministry. I'm telling you: If you focus on the children and youth, everything you need for God's vision for the broader ministry of your church will come. Placing youth and children's ministries at the forefront of priority (in action and not just lip service) will draw the families—younger leadership, fresh ideas, strong backs, and energy! By spreading limited resources over a wide ministry menu of "something for everyone," too many smaller churches don't do anything really well. (You could make a similar statement about some larger churches making the same mistake, but that's a conversation for another author in another book!)

THOUGHT #14

Is your smaller church missing the point?

Selling your youth ministry vision can be tough in a smaller church. It goes back to that "everybody just knows" way of thinking about a church's purpose, plan, and people-target. Many smaller churches lack a strategic plan for their ministry today and a vision for the future. So, when a smart youth minister presents an exciting, comprehensive vision for the youth ministry, it can be met with a blank "whatever you want to do" attitude. Underlying tension can also exist because what you're doing as youth leader may be more progressive than what your leadership is doing overall.

John (from thought #11) must feel passionately about this subject because he has something to say here, too:

"In the almost five years I've been at Eastview, I've watched our student ministry demographic change from mostly churched teenagers to mostly unchurched ones. Many of these kids are the needy ones from broken families, where

under-employment and unemployment are rampant. Along the way, we've faced resistance from parents and other 'concerned' adults about 'those kids' coming to church. We've stuck to our guns and watched some families leave. I have worked hard to equip our leaders in ministering to these teenagers, we've read books together, and our leaders have fallen in love with the students other churches kicked out. The key for us has been patience and communication about the needs and challenges these teenagers face. It's paid off this past summer. We got 10 kids to our church camp through an 'adopt a kid' program; it wouldn't have been possible without the church's buy-in financially."

THOUGHT #15

Breaking the "small church mentality"

Kill the phrase, "But we're just a small church."

Here's how fellow youth pastor Keith White from Lost Mountain Baptist Church in Powder Springs, Georgia, remembers his teenage years:

"Growing up in a small church with a small youth group, relationships were all that we had. Today, the group I work with is much larger, with the full-on light-and-sound experience. From knowing how incredible those relationships were growing up, smaller groups and

relationships have formed out of our larger group. Years from now, I don't want the youth of today to remember how great the lights were. I want them to tell me that I made a difference in their lives, like the difference so many people made in my life years ago."

THOUGHT #16

When *not* to think big

Jeremiah 29:11 shares how God tells us, *"I know the plans I have for you."* So, what if your church wants to plan on staying small? I've heard church leaders say things like, "I don't want us to grow. I like our smaller size." Personally, I don't think we get to decide. Who we are as a ministry is God's call. All he's asked from us is to be faithful and "go into the world." We don't get the luxury of saying, "We've reached the goal of XX number of students in our youth program. We can stop our outreach now."

But if it's clear to your leadership that you're exactly where God wants you in size, go with it. *Please* don't compare yourself to the mega-ministry down the street. When people compare your ministry to someone else's, gently educate them on the benefits of a smaller group.

THOUGHT #17

How to counterbalance the big/small debate

Did you know that according to the National Congregations Study (soc.duke.edu/natcong), the average size youth group in America is about eight students? It shocks churchy folks when they hear that even in the era of megachurches, the average size church in America is 76 people.

Jon Batch, a youth guy from Cincinnati, Ohio, had this to say:

"I was hired by the little church in town, thinking I was doing big ministry. We were doing good things, seeing kids come to Christ and growing…only to have core students come to church excited about the even bigger church's all-nighter, paintball, blow-up games event. It was a blow to the pride, knowing that one church spent equal to my year's budget on one event.

"The answer I came to took about six years, but here it is: I realized it didn't matter how my ministry compared to the 'Big Dog' down the street, but how effective my ministry was. I had the opportunity to take fewer teens and invest in them as much as I could."

Rejoice in who you are, and cheerlead all the fabulous work God is doing in the lives of your students. Educate your church leadership about the reality of smaller church youth ministry. You'll be giving them a balanced outlook and expectation for your ministry effectiveness. Your education efforts also will keep them from putting too much of the responsibility of attracting younger families onto the shoulders of your ministry alone.

THOUGHT #18   Re-imagine and re-image

Marketing your ministry begins within the walls of your worship. Your greatest publicity posters are the faces of the people in your parish passing on the positive points of your purpose and passion. (Yeah, I just got on an alliterative roll with the letter "p.")

Be intentional about recruiting a few people who make sure your ministry paints an upbeat, hopeful buzz to the rest of the congregation. Create a verbal marketing team that includes one or two of the key older folks, a couple of visibly active parents, one or two pivotal people on the leadership board, a person involved in your church's mission efforts, and people from other key areas particular to your church. These individuals would not actually have to do any tangible marketing with brochures, posters, or announcements—though that would help on occasion. Instead, their job is simply to praise what the youth ministry is doing and find ways to make connecting points between the people in the congregation and your ministry.

THOUGHT #19

Invite the big dogs into your pound

I'm talking "big dogs" on two levels: the bigger youth ministry churches and the church leaders within your church itself. There's no need for a complete separation of "us vs. them" attitude.

Leaders from bigger church youth ministries can be your friends. They're a great connection for borrowing stuff your ministry doesn't have, or they can provide places to stay when you need an overnight retreat location. Do you need a worship leader or speaker to add some "sizzle to the steak" of an upcoming youth event? Bigger churches will have several adults that aren't the primary youth pastor but can fit the bill for your event and are usually thrilled to be asked. Ask if the bigger group can adopt your smaller group for big events that you couldn't do otherwise, such as retreats, concerts, camps, and mission projects.

One word of advice: If you do join a bigger church for a few events, make sure that your students and leaders still have ownership and an area or two of significant responsibility. It keeps both groups cognizant of one another's needs and gifts.

It's also smart to create connections between your ministry and your church leaders, inviting them into your world. Sometimes church leaders need a gentle reminder that the youth are also a part of their constituency. Students are not the church of the future; at any point on a church's time continuum, students are a part of the church of today.

So which people am I talking about and what should they do? The folks I have in mind are the senior pastor, the board chairperson, the church secretary, and key finance and property people. I can tell you this much: Do *not* invite them to something where they just sit off by themselves or lean against the wall. Prepare them in advance for ways to mix with your students, and give each person something significant to do, such as taking tickets at the door, helping serve a special meal, being a driver (and singer!) when Christmas caroling to the shut-ins, or hosting a pool party or movie night.

THOUGHT #20

Running with *the* Big Dog

This thought wasn't part of my original outline, but God has a powerful way of working through my fingers to add, delete, and correct my thoughts. God's the ultimate editor!

Please don't make some of the mistakes I did earlier in my ministry career and fall into the "glory trap" that often comes with moving up the ministry size ladder. Oh, we don't talk about it in polite circles—but many of us think it. "The bigger my ministry, the bigger youth pastor deal I am." I remember when a former group of mine reached my magic number of

100. There was an attitude about it—almost like a "Delta Medallion Member" elite club status. I started getting asked to do more speaking for other groups, and other groups came more often to watch what I was doing—as if the number of teenagers in my group automatically made me an expert on all things youth ministry.

If you follow that line of reasoning, does working with smaller church youth groups mean I'm less of an "expert" than before? Does it minimize what you do with your students? Of course not! Great youth ministry has a one-on-one focus to it—one teenager at a time in your line of sight. Changes everything, doesn't it? Whether you have 10 or 100 or 1,000, it's still only one teenager at a time. Levels the unspoken playing field. Equalizes the effectiveness measuring stick. Always remember how important your students are and that they deserve the best and that's you.

Here's what *the* ultimate Big Dog has to say for being faithful to his plans: *"Well done, my good and faithful servant!" (Matthew 25:23).*

the vortex of volunteers

Everyone in my church is already doing everything!

Yeah, that's a problem. It's what happens in smaller churches. But it happens in larger churches, too. You've probably heard of the 80/20 Rule before: 20 percent of the people do 80 percent of the work. It seems even more epidemic in smaller churches where people have all the desire in the world to accomplish big things, but fewer legs to pull it all together.

But I'm unwilling to accept that ministry has to be this way. My experience says that it's not that people won't volunteer; instead, I think we lean toward the easy "yes" people (like our friends) over and over again. We don't always take the time to think outside of the recruiting box. When we narrow our "ask list" world, we shortchange our ministries of fresh insights and life-blood.

Broaden your scope of the people you ask to volunteer by making a job task list. Match your tasks with the names of people who are good at those sorts of things. Include those admin items you never seem to have time for, such as decorating bulletin boards, setting up supplies for Sunday school classes, and inventorying the leftover Fall Festival goodies.

Smaller church youth ministry volunteer recruiting is hard!

Putting together a team of "week in and week out" volunteers doesn't work like it does in larger churches.

The percentages work against a smaller church youth ministry. You don't have a large pool of people to draw from, so the likelihood of running across a dormant youth worker who wants to volunteer on your team is somewhere between nil and none. (Though it could happen. I was doing a Youth Ministry Architects consultation in a church that needed more volunteers and met a 30-ish guy who'd joined the church six months previously, wrote down that he wanted to volunteer in the youth ministry, but had never been asked!)

Yes, it's harder to find the volunteers with the skill sets your ministry needs. What to do? Make good decisions about what your ministry needs. Make sure your volunteers are serving from their giftedness. Maybe the answer will be that some of your volunteers serve in a dual capacity like Driver Coordinator and Small Group Leader. On the other end of the spectrum, breaking down the volunteer needs into small chunks will attract and involve more people. The bonus in that is that it also sets up your team for long-term sustainability. You end up with a healthier team and less burnout.

Here's a story of volunteer burnout from Justin Dougan, who serves as a volunteer youth director:

"After one youth service, I led a small group that included two girls who were fighting over a guy. They repeatedly interrupted my discussion until I boiled over. I said a few things a youth pastor should never say.

"So with the stress of 1) little to no budget, 2) several long-time volunteers who had just quit, 3) my strenuous day job, and 4) the episode that had just taken place, I realized I was burning out in a blaze of glory. I already had my mental resignation letter written and was just waiting to spring it on the leadership.

"The leaders wanted me to get training but then decided the church couldn't afford it. So God orchestrated what only he can! I received a phone call from Dennis Beckner at volunteeryouthministry.com, who told me I had been selected to receive a free trip to the Simply Youth Ministry Conference! God reaffirmed his calling in me and healed my

wounded, burnt spirit. I know God can still use me to leave a lasting mark on the lives of students."

THOUGHT #23

Just like *America's Got Talent*!

You ever watch that show? It starts off with loads of "interesting" (and by that, I mean "weird") people trying out for the title. There's an open call for "anything goes," from opera singers who knit hats to the human dressed as a toe to the guy who sneezes on command. It wouldn't be so much fun if we didn't get to watch the judges ring in with their X's signaling their dissatisfaction with the performance. Since summer TV is bad anyway, I've found myself glued to the set wondering what oddity will appear next. One word? Fun!

Does an open casting call work well in recruiting volunteers? Uhhhhh…no. Unlike the TV show, you may have a tough time finding the button that eliminates the less-than-desirable volunteers once they're in place. Getting rid of poor volunteers is difficult and emotional, plus it can be a political pothole. Better to never let "bad acts" onto your youth ministry stage from the get-go.

Here's a story from my friend Scott Cohoon from Plainwell, Michigan, about a youth ministry volunteer who was not prepared to lead in a good way:

"Our church youth group was part of a multiple-church missions week. The purpose was to work on housing remodeling during the day, then worship and activities together at night for several days. It also required overnight stays, which meant girls were in one church and guys in another. Anyway, there was one particular young man that had been getting on everyone's nerves all week for multiple reasons. On one of the last nights several of the older students were looking for a way to 'get even' with this young man. The volunteer became aware of their plans of 'revenge' and rather than use the opportunity for explaining the reasons not to engage in their plans, helped them accomplish their plan. So, before you knew it they had a middle school boy duct taped to a tree. Not the greatest volunteer moment."

So avoid making announcements that beg for people to fill key spots where a volunteer has lots of potential for quality interaction with your students. There should *never* be a cattle call for small group leaders, class teachers, summer trip adults—events where developing and deepening Christ-like mentoring relationships is optimal. Open calls are OK for things like drivers, food preparation, and movie theater chaperones, but not for your core team.

Finding the right volunteers

I mentioned "making a list" in thought #21, but I want to flesh out the process a little more. Here's a quick-step process that works for me:

1) Make a list of *every* job/task that needs doing in your ministry.

2) Connect any items that should/could be lumped together. For example, the same person who changes the bulletin boards could make your posters. Someone who likes to plan holiday events for your students also might like to decorate your youth space.

3) Write up a job description for each job on your list. Include ministry description, expectations, goals, plans, outcomes, spiritual impacts, and resources available. Explain that all volunteers are required to undergo a background check and safety training.

4) Grab your church directory and your job list. Go through the directory and pencil in names to fit each job. Don't assume they're too busy or will say no.

5) Always focus on "inviting them" to serve and not that you're desperate for help.

6) Send a personal letter or e-mail to each person on your list; include the information about the specific role you'd like this person to consider. Ask people not to respond for seven days but instead be in prayer about it. Make sure that you let them know you are available for more info and that you will also be praying for those seven days.

7) Call people at the end of the week to compare notes on the Spirit's guidance. The cream will have risen to the top of who says yes and who says no, and if they didn't pray, then they may not be the people you needed anyway.

THOUGHT #25

Do those background checks

You *must* do background checks. That's it. Just do them. You need to put the whole safe sanctuary scenario into action in your youth and children's ministries.

You may be thinking, "We're a small church. I know everybody." Yes, it may seem like a hassle, but you'd be surprised who will show up. I know two youth workers close to me who ran background checks and found registered sex offenders who were in their church membership and were circling around their youth ministries.

After you've gone through the recruiting process and volunteers have said "yes," have them fill out an application that covers both child protection policies and fun personal info. Do this before people start serving. Also require that everyone attend a child protection training; many in-house training models are available. Check with your church's denominational leadership.

THOUGHT #26

"What we have here is a failure to communicate"

Youth workers express frustration over finding good volunteers—and volunteers frequently express frustration about the quality and effectiveness of their leaders. So what does a good leader provide?

Consistent communication is paramount. Establish a few communication ground rule basics for your team:

1) What's the best form of communication for your volunteers? Is it Facebook®, e-mail, text, or (heaven forbid!) a phone call tree?

2) What needs to be communicated to the volunteer team? Topics could include that week's lesson plans, small group discussion questions, and the schedule for that week's youth service.

3) How often will you communicate that content? Will it be weekly, monthly, on a specific day of the week, and so on?

4) What is a volunteer's responsibility in checking the communication you send and staying informed, and what's the best way for a volunteer to communicate ideas, thoughts, needs, and feedback to you?

THOUGHT #27

Train them in the way they should go

You've constructed an amazing team! Look around—wow! Your recruiting work is done. Now you're ready to roll up your sleeves and get to ministry, right?

Not quite. Your team needs training and direction. Never assume that your people have all the youth ministry answers. A good leader provides training opportunities, such as taking volunteers to a one-day training event or bringing in an outside speaker to do a training event for your team. (Remember that partnering with a bigger church thing? This is a good spot for it.) Provide a few solid books for volunteers to sharpen their youth ministry skills; *Help! I'm a Volunteer Youth Worker* is still a valuable classic—or maybe give them copies of this book! If nothing else, get each team member a subscription to GROUP Magazine. It's like every youth leader's "how-to" manual.

THOUGHT #28

You've claimed and trained a team; now maintain

Want to make a difference for Jesus in the lives of your students? It starts with you and your adult leaders. I want you to take a deep look inside your ministry. Who gets the biggest chunk of your ministry attention? Your students or your adults?

Think about how Jesus built his earthly ministry. Most of his three-year "church staff job" time was spent with his "volunteer leadership team," the 12 disciples. Now, look at your average ministry week and how you spend your time. Will the youth ministry police come after me if I suggest that your largest chunk of weekly ministry time should be spent in developing your leaders? There's some "doing more with less" right there. Since there's less of you, you multiply the ministry effectiveness to students around you by directly investing more time in your adults than in your students. (True, maybe it's a "quiet" investment so your students don't get their feelings in a wad.)

Obviously, I don't mean you never spend time with students. Just keep it all in balance, with the greater percentage spent on the volunteers. Included in this time are your written communications about each week's lessons, coffee chats, prayer for each team member, affirmations (verbal and gifts), equipping/info meetings, training, coaching, and maybe even a small group study together. You get the idea.

"It's all about relationships. Each of us has a capacity for a limited number of relationships. Having a smaller youth group and smaller volunteer team is a virtual guarantee that I can have genuine relationships with most of my students and adult volunteers." —Dusty Smith; Immanuel Baptist Church; Marshall, Texas.

THOUGHT #29

While we're on the subject of volunteer affirmations...

Some of us are better at this than others. I love doing affirmation projects and surprises for my team. It brings me so much joy, and I feel like it's been a reason for my success in the volunteer arena.

Want a list of easy-to-do affirmations?

1) **Flock the Flock's Leaders:** Have students each make a stick-sign (heart-shaped ones work great at Valentine's Day), then sneak up in the volunteer's yard. Making a quick getaway before being discovered is most of the fun. Don't worry, the neighbors will let your volunteer know they've been flocked!

2) **Candy Corn Caper:** Cover a volunteer's car with real candy corn or candy corn colored

streamers. Have the students sign and leave a card that says, "Thanks for planting God's Word into our lives."

3) **Flower Delivery:** This one seems weird, but it doesn't have to be. Churches and funeral homes have flowers left over from weddings and funerals. Take their leftovers, make new arrangements in vases you got at the church yard sale, and go on a flower delivery to your team member's front doors. No need to tell them where the flowers came from!

4) **Remember their birthdays:** Come on! Even Facebook® helps you with this one. It's as simple as a birthday card mailed to your volunteer's house. Getting mail still goes a long way.

5) **Volunteer Care Packages:** This is sort of like a care package for college students—only fill it with youth trip necessities like breath mints, tissues, ear plugs, candy, travel toiletries, and so on.

While we're on the subject of volunteer spiritual growth…

A team that grows together spiritually is a team that goes together in the Spirit. It's hard to take our teenagers where we as leaders aren't, right? Each volunteer must be walking close to God in worship and word, and your team's impact will be even greater if you came from the same spiritual page.

This is much more easily said than done! Here's one idea to accomplish this in multiple ways; find what works for your leaders. Study and discuss the upcoming or previous week's youth lesson:

> 1) In an online chat room.
>
> 2) In an ongoing "reply all" e-mail.
>
> 3) On Skype®!
>
> 4) On a late-night conference call from wherever.
>
> 5) About 45 minutes before (or after) your youth group night.
>
> 6) As a Sunday school class.
>
> 7) In a different home each week.
>
> 8) In the same home each week.

9) Where else? Starbucks®!

10) At the minimum, provide study material or devotions to do at home.

it's a balancing act...

THOUGHT #31

...with your God

We're in ministry, right? We talk and study about God all the time, right? So God is always numero uno on our priority list, right? Who are we kidding? You and I both know that preparing a few ministry lessons each week does not a relationship with God make.

Let me help you take a personal soul inventory:

1) When was the last time you read the Bible and it had *nothing* to do with any church or ministry obligations?

2) How often do you sit through the entire weekly worship service without missing a portion because of some ministry-related chore?

3) When did you last worship "somewhere else" where you had no responsibilities except showing up and worshiping God?

4) How often do you sit for more than 10 minutes and allow God to quietly talk to you?

"All too seldom." "Not often enough." That's what I thought. Me, too. I'll let you finish up this thought from here by spending a few minutes alone with God.

THOUGHT #32 ...with your family

Family time always comes first. That's one of the most basic politically correct statements at church, isn't it? I'm convinced that some church workers make sure they are overheard making such comments, thereby boosting how others perceive their ministry effectiveness. Unfortunately, the reality is that all too many ministry families suffer lives of quiet desperation.

A typical smaller church mentality doesn't help make that better, either. The church can barely afford the staff it has, so in the back of the leaders' collective minds, they're thinking "We've got to get the most we can out of this guy or girl." Somehow there's an unspoken justification that if your family is at church *with* you all those too many hours, that counts as quality family time. Hahahahahahahahaha! That's funny! (Not so much.)

Gently and lovingly but firmly educate, inform, or remind your leadership that family time is time spent "off church property." How you spend it is your business; three or more nights a week at church does not create good family boundaries and is a warning sign of danger ahead. Being a preacher's kid, I can remember resenting my dad's time away at church. I don't remember ever playing with my dad. Is that the memory you want for your kids? I didn't think so.

"I love that 'making my family my first ministry' can be more than a talking point in a smaller church. I know it might not be this way everywhere, but I have more time with my family than I ever did in a larger church. Plus my kids are known, appreciated, and ministered to...sometimes simply because they're my kids." —Darren Sutton; Christ Point Church; Corpus Christi, Texas

THOUGHT #33   ...with your soul

My friend Jana Snyder is a youth pastor, author, retreat speaker, and woman-extraordinaire. She lives is Richfield, Pennsylvania, where she and her husband serve a local church. She expresses this next thought so much better than I ever could.

"From my experience, ministry can be soul-sucking at times. (Can I say that?) I used to work in a church with a great and

*growing youth ministry. Families were joining the church,
many of them because their teenagers were involved in the
youth ministry.*

*"Yet I was dying emotionally. It felt like every time I walked
into the office following a great youth camping or missions
trip, I'd find a letter in my mailbox from the pastor listing all
the things I had done wrong on that trip or event. He never
talked directly to me about any of these things; it was always
letters in my mailbox or at my once-a-year review with the
personnel committee and I'd get a written bashing by the
pastor. I was always devastated. I thought I was doing a
great job since lives were being changed. Yet the politics of
the church were winning out. My soul hurt!*

*"My solution? I felt strongly that I needed to honor the pastor
as my boss (and as the pastor) and I didn't want to gossip
(very hard to do). So I found a small group from another
church in town, which allowed me a place to share and
receive some much-needed soul care."*

THOUGHT #34 ...with your ministry

Does this sound at all familiar? It's the week before a major
church holiday. Your church to-do list includes these tasks:
driving the seniors to their holiday luncheon, decorating
the hallways for the upcoming holiday, helping serve at the

church's version of the holiday meal, attending four holiday school concerts, rehearsing for said holiday's cantata because the choir needed an extra singer, working the sound for the children's holiday skit, and making a dish for the obligatory staff version of the holiday meal. Oh, and actually meeting with your students and perhaps having enough energy left to explain why this holiday hubbub is so important to their eternal salvation. Makes very little complete sense now that we look at it this way, does it?

"Working at a smaller church, I sometimes get sucked into other responsibilities that don't pertain to youth work. That's why I had to learn how to say 'no' and focus on my ministry responsibilities, including the dreaded admin work! For me, I've found that when I fail to do the organizational stuff, meetings don't get planned, parents are not as informed, and students fall through the cracks. So...I do my admin work first thing in the morning. When I do this consistently, my ministry benefits tremendously!" —Tom Pounder; New Life Christian Church; Chantilly, Virginia

THOUGHT #35

...with your job(s)

More from Jana Snyder:

"One of the traps I fell into during my early years of ministry was the trap of feeling like there was always more to do

(which there was) and I had to do everything. With that mentality, I was headed for certain burnout.

"Want some advice? Find a few other 'survivor' youth leaders who have survived ministry longer than you. I've had great sounding boards from ministry people who have gone through their own rough times."

And for those of you who work a full- or part-time job out in the "real world" so you can afford to do this youth ministry thing? God bless you! You're a special kind of youth worker. There are Cracker Barrel rocking chairs on God's front porch waiting for you in heaven, and today's full-time youth pastors will bring you lemonade on demand.

THOUGHT
#36   ...with your boss

I've had the full spectrum of relationships with bosses, from awesome to not-so-hot. It's a balancing act for me; I'm an independent thinker who asks for forgiveness more than I ask for permission.

When you're serving in a smaller church, it's a normal dynamic to work independently. You don't get to see your boss, church leadership, or other staff members regularly. Depending on the hours you put in, you're often not keeping office hours when everyone else does. So how do you avoid an out-of-balance ministry boss relationship? I call it "full disclosure."

Here's what I do: Everything goes into an e-mail and everything gets CC'd to my boss/pastor. This accomplishes several things: 1) I summarize my ministry conversations with people so everyone's working off the same page; 2) I let my boss know what I'm accomplishing, which provides a sense of the time I'm putting in; and 3) There are no surprises. (Bosses hate surprises!)

THOUGHT #37

...with your time

When I asked fellow youth pastor Mark Cox from Bryant, Arkansas, to share his thoughts on time management, here is what he said: *"By my own admission, I'm not a good time manager. In fact, I'm a horrible time manager. I know this, because when crunch time hits on big projects, I end up saying the same thing every time: 'Why didn't I take care of that issue weeks ago?' Help!"* I love Mark's honesty.

I would consider myself a great time manager. But having just typed this paragraph while behind on my deadline for this chapter, maybe I'm not so good. I'd say I'm better than most. When we're working in a smaller church setting, we have less time to waste. Every second counts because there's no room in the schedule for do-overs without something else tumbling out of balance.

What works for me? I follow this principle: "Handle a piece of paper only once." I learned that at a time-management seminar too many years ago. It's an electronic world now, but the principle still applies. When it comes across your desk or computer screen, deal with it once and right away. Period.

THOUGHT #38

...with your week

Develop a healthy pattern for those all-important seven days. Schedule time frames for what's most important. Here's a suggested order: God, marriage, family, personal, home, job, youth ministry, other church needs, dishes. Just sayin'.

I asked Jana to share this workweek story of hers:

"I was working more than 80 hours a week, without taking any time for myself, no day off, a 24-7 pace. I was beginning to run ragged. That's when I took three pieces of great advice from a few 'lifers' in youth ministry:

> *1) I took a day off weekly. I made it known that it was my day off. I turned off my phone and did the things that I wanted to do (or caught up on laundry and dishes).*

2) *I looked at my day in three time slots: morning, afternoon, and evening. If I had an event or youth group in the evening, then I would pick either the morning or the afternoon slot to take off. Way too often I would work all day in the office then go to youth group, tired and worn out.*

3) *Lastly, I changed my mindset. It is not my job to save kids. It's God's job to change their lives, and I'm just his tool. My job is to love and invest in students, preparing an environment for God to work within. It was a life-changing moment for me."*

THOUGHT #39

...with your organization

Do your ministry and students a favor: If you're not organized, find someone who is. Your ministry world would run so much smoother if you stopped trying to be Superman or Wonder Woman and instead let someone else put your operating systems into place.

I know you. You need to give that person a list, don't you? Rock that person's world by delivering this list:

- Update youth database of students and families' contact info
- Set up student/parent mailing label templates

- Get all the right e-mail addresses into the right e-mail groups
- Format texting groups: middle school, senior high, parents, volunteers, and so on
- Update the website (I checked your web page, and we're all sick of looking at pics from last year's youth retreat)
- Create and maintain an online youth calendar that everyone can access in a read-only format

And your office? Oh believe me, there's a mom *dying* to clean that pigsty. Go ahead and let 'er.

THOUGHT #40

...with your free time

I'm preaching to the choir here, or the pot calling the kettle black—some tired cliché. I like to work; it's fun. I really like what I do: talking with youth workers all over. So I have my own room for growth in this particular area.

Still, I need to "play" more. I've lost count of all the movies I couldn't wait to be released—but then I didn't see them in the theater. (I don't even keep up with the movies when they come out "on demand" right to my TV.) I need to spend time at Starbucks® with friends who aren't in ministry. Or read James Patterson's latest book. Or meander the local mall I haven't visited since moving to Houston—and it's less than a mile away.

And sometimes it's OK to just do nothing. Who do I see about making that happen?

the particulars on parents

You can't ignore parents

Parents are a necessary evil of youth ministry. OK, they're not evil. (Usually.) I'm kidding! (Mostly.) After all, I'm a parent myself.

Numerous studies done by researchers at places like Gallup, Barna, Search Institute, and GROUP Magazine have revealed overwhelming evidence proving that parents remain the No. 1 "faith influencers" in the lives of teenagers today. In both positive and negative ways, parents are the major molding influence, not the youth pastor.

What does that mean to you and me? If you don't minister to the parents, you won't be as effective in ministering to their children. So embrace the parents in your ministry. Don't see them as stumbling blocks, but view them as both the corner and capstone of the foundation you're laying down in the lives of your students.

Parents can be critics

Generally, parents will rate your youth leader effectiveness based solely on their child's experience within the program. If their teenager likes it, parents like you. If their teenager hates the program and would rather be somewhere else or is truly *the* weirdest kid you've ever met, parents will still think you must be the problem. Apparently, you stink as a youth pastor.

Keep that in mind. It makes it easier to understand where a parent's head is when that person is in your office wondering why Johnny won't stop playing the latest top-selling violent video game to come to your youth group. Parents desperately want their children to fit in and be loved within a healthy, positive group of people. They desperately want more God for their teenagers, but most don't have the equipping skills to make that significant investment. They (albeit unfairly) look to you to provide their student with the God-stuff.

By the way, sometimes what parents have to say is right on the money. They have a wisdom, insight and experience that you may not. Learning when to listen is a "must have" skill for a youth pastor who wants to make it for the long haul.

THOUGHT #43

Parents can be communication consumers

Parents are grownups, right? They don't need to hear every detail five different ways, right? They'll open that letter you sent out in September and diligently follow the timeline you carefully laid out, right? Of course they won't. They're busy—sometimes too busy!

Scott Cohoon from First Baptist Church in Plainwell, Michigan, had a communication problem. Here's what he did:

"Communication with parents is my biggest challenge. Since fliers never seem to make it home, I have to be creative for finding ways to connect with parents.

"Two successful ideas have worked for me: First, I meet the parents in the parking lot after an event or youth group night. I just chat without hurrying to get home and the TV show-du-jour.

"The second one is a bit more creative, my 'Anything for a $1' challenge. I called each student's parents with a list of 10 questions about their teenager. I got to know parents I normally don't talk with. At youth group, I used those answers to quiz our group to guess who I was talking about. A correct guess earned a dollar for whichever student correctly answered. If they didn't guess correctly, the student I was reading about got the $1."

53

What simple and fun ways to get to know parents and introduce yourself as a humble ally in the nurturing of their teenager's faith walk.

Parents can be absent

I once came back from a middle school trip and did the whole parent pick-up thing, only to realize I had one student left over. She stayed with me for the next two days while we hunted down her parents to say, "Uh, we're back. Pick up your anxious teenager!" So I know how frustrating it can be to feel like your youth program is a "drop-off" service for adults who want Parents' Night Out—or Parents' Weekend Out!

Absentee parents are a part of the deal. You can be frustrated about it all you want, but it's not going to help anything. My suggestion is that you intentionally pursue connecting points with parents who aren't as connected to the ministry as you wish they were. Ideas include:

1) Take Scott's idea from thought #43 and chat with parents at drop-off or pick-up times.

2) Use snail mail. These parents won't read the bulletin or church e-mail because they probably

aren't in church, and you'll be lucky to get their e-mail address.

3) If you only have so much time for phone calls, absent parents are the ones you want to spend time calling. Praise their teenager, get to know them as people, build a relationship. Find ways to gently speak God into their lives and show them who the church really is.

THOUGHT #45

Parents can be volunteers

Scott Cohoon is a really smart, wise youth worker. Here's more insight:

"I believe the best way to have a strong team is to utilize parents in their natural areas of strengths. One way we go about that is to have an outline when it comes to events. I will have some ideas in print with timeframes and a list of potential questions or problems to work through. Finally, I include potential 'job descriptions' we need filled, giving parents opportunities to step into areas of interest."

Are you familiar with the "I can't volunteer because I'm a parent" myth? Just a lame excuse from parents who don't want to step up—or youth workers who are afraid to recruit them. Parents are adults who were once teenagers.

Believe it or not, giving birth did not automatically remove the twisted gene that makes them effective at relating to teenagers.

Obviously, some of your students don't want their mom or dad leading their small group. I wouldn't set it up that way. Use some discretion in where you involve parents of students within the ministry scope of the group. Use them with middle schoolers if their teenager is in high school. Set up behavioral boundaries for volunteer parents and their teenagers while at youth events.

Our youngest daughter used to make me drop her off a block from the church so she could walk in and not be seen arriving with me. Whatever. Imagine my responses when she asked for money.

Involving parents on my youth ministry volunteer team has always worked great for me. Parents are already there, with many just dying to be asked. Use them wisely.

THOUGHT
#46

Parents can provide support

Want parents to be supportive? Support them back. Parents have two overarching needs from you as their child's youth pastor: First, love their child; and second, communicate— often and early!

To take the concept further in garnering parental support, intentionally recruit and utilize parents who "get you" and the ministry. Invite them into the ministry as people who positively market its blessings to other parents. In addition, find parents who love you, and ask them to hold you accountable to any ministry areas in which you're struggling. Also find parents who are there for you when you need a shoulder to lean on, have a meal, take care of your kids, call at a sudden emergency, and so on. This type of parent is the one who keeps you going when other parents are giving you a rough time.

THOUGHT #47 Parents can provide resources

Parents bring all kinds of gifts to the youth ministry meal counter. Some of them have time to volunteer, some can run the kitchen, some have money to spend on the program, and some have great connections or stuff your ministry needs.

At the beginning of each school year (or as new students join the group during the year), have parents fill out an info sheet. Ask them what they have that your ministry might be able to borrow. It could be stuff like a boat, a cabin in the woods, box seats at the stadium, and so on. Also ask parents what they do and if there's anything their profession or company can bring to the ministry in freebies or donations. Ideas might include corporate sponsorship, free makeovers, or an endless supply of Skittles. You get the idea. Do your research so you can dream up interesting ways to utilize parents' connections.

THOUGHT #48   Parents can be your friends

No matter your age, parents of your students *can* be your friends. I would go so far as to say that it's a savvy, shrewd move on your part to purposefully strive to make friends with parents, stopping short of being an unhealthy people-pleaser.

I've consulted in too many churches where the youth leader had it right *and* wrong about parents. Many youth workers get it right in developing relationships with the students; they miss the mark by not realizing the equal importance of relational ministry to Mom and Dad. This is a mistake most often made by younger youth workers, and it's understandable.

When you're a young youth worker, you have less in common with the older parents of your students. Don't be afraid, but don't act cocky. Just walk humbly with a servant attitude. You'll lose respect from parents when you act like you know it all. You'll gain respect when you listen to and consider parents' perspectives.

For all of us no matter our age in ministry, plan fun times with parents. Have youth parent game night. Schedule a youth group night where your students baby-sit all the other younger kids while you and the parents experience a typical youth group night. Go on coffee chats with parents. The idea is to get to know them and let them get to know you— and your ministry will be stronger for it. When hard times come, and they will, those parents will be standing beside you.

Parents can be enemies

You've probably heard the old saying "Keep your friends close and your enemies closer." Wikipedia attributes it to an ancient Chinese general, Sun Tzu, in 400 B.C. A general— how appropriate.

Some of you may want to chastise me for talking about parents as enemies, but I've had a few. I didn't start it! (I look forward to your letters.) Maybe no one would call themselves my mortal enemy, but from my 30 years of youth ministry, one couple comes to mind that I'm not sure would call 911 if I caught on fire. Yeah, they didn't like me. No worries; they're too busy burning me in effigy to be reading this book.

Not every parent has to like you. But I was too naïve to realize the extent of these parents' feelings toward me, and I didn't guard myself. What I should have done was work harder at surrounding myself with people who could keep this couple's fiery darts from hitting me so often. I mean, it's gonna happen in ministry but I could have been a lot wiser in being aware. Ah, you live and learn—at the next church.

THOUGHT #50

Help parents become people of God

In your ministry, parents probably struggle as much in faith issues as their teenagers do. Be sensitive to that, and pray for a passion for the lives of your moms and dads. Pray with them, invite them into holy moments of encountering God, give them resources to fertilize their faith, and be a witness to them of the mighty love of a God who loves them as much as he loves their children. Minister to the parent, and you've ministered to the teenager.

the oddities of a smaller group

It might be odd, but it's great!

I've said it before, but I'm going to say it again: I love the advantages of having a smaller youth ministry. Here's what a few friends had to say when I asked them to share why they liked working with a smaller number of students:

- Jason Underwood: *"I love being able to invest in individual students rather than just the group. I like to spend time with that 'Timothy' student and see how God puts them to work."*
- Haley Wherry: *"Being able to know what's going on in each student's life. Being able to remember everyone's name! Most every student is at the same school, which makes it easier to invest in their campus."*
- Amanda Weirick: *"A few words come to mind: intimacy, insight, and spontaneity. You gain intimacy in smaller group setting, a bond, closeness, a deepness, and connectedness. Ultimately you gain their trust. You gain insight into the lives of your students."*

- Drew Aaron: *"It forces you to remain creative because you don't have the other resources that attract kids."*
- Will Gregg: *"With small youth groups we get a chance to know everyone and what they are going through. We can create more efficient and directed lessons to impact the students in their situations."*
- Missy Yingling Watson: *"I love being able to lend my own personal minivan as the new church van for mission trips. Feeling valued by having lots of slashes in my title."*
- Lauren Brown Surprenant: *"Building on what Haley said, by knowing your students, you can tell when they have that 'look' like something is bothering them. You just know when they need extra love and care. And impromptu field trips 'cuz they all fit in a van or two is a close second fav."*

THOUGHT
#52

Yes, some students can be odd

Things can get out of balance with a smaller size group; sometimes the smaller the number, the odder the—well, the oddness.

First of all, with a smaller group, different personality types stick out more. This dynamic can spell trouble. If you have someone in your group whose social or physical makeup makes it tougher for group acceptance, there aren't as many ways for that teenager to hide among the masses, and you probably don't have other students with that same personality.

On the other hand, smaller groups can make it easier to welcome in the unusual student—with a little guidance from you. Stress the importance of how people in the group can care for one another. Create opportunities for your students to agree on how they treat and respect one another. Find specific, purposeful ways for "the hard to fit in" teenager to serve and discover her niche. All of this will equip your students with the capacity for unconditional love.

THOUGHT #53

Deal with odd ways of teaching

I get asked this a lot: "How do you effectively teach a Sunday School class or Bible study when there's a sixth-grade boy, two eighth-grade giggly girls, a freshman boy, and a senior in high school? What curriculum is there for that?"

Great question. On one hand, you face the problem of meeting multiple age-level learning needs if you keep them together—but then there's the "awkward turtle" factor of a lack of critical mass if you split them up into even smaller groups. Yikes! What to do?

Get more creative by providing learning that encourages experiential, self-discovery experiences. The group can walk through a learning activity together, but debrief it in smaller, more appropriate age-level pairs or groups of three. Journaling is another great way to provide a place for your students to God-process their learning from the lesson of the day.

Another shift in thinking from the typical Sunday morning or Wednesday night Bible study model is to use your corporate gathering times for more relational bonding and friendship building. Partner that with focused times for a cup of coffee or a soda with smaller groups of your students, matched according to their learning needs. That becomes the time when the spiritual learning can happen based on where they are emotionally and developmentally.

THOUGHT #54

Get ready for those odd activities

Some youth events just won't work with smaller numbers of students. For example, a youth-sponsored pumpkin patch can be tough with only five teenagers in the group. Or what about those places that require minimum numbers to participate or get the better group prices? Pulling off a production of *Godspell* with seven students could be tough, especially if you have only one guy and he can't sing a note.

So our smaller-size group activity planning has to be appropriate. I just had a Facebook® conversation with a middle school youth director in North Carolina. She was stressing out because she didn't have the 10 teenagers she needed for a weekend event and wondered what she should do.

Plan well and plan ahead. Make plans that take advantage of your group size. For example, one of my students is big time into stage production of musicals at his specialty school. His plays are scheduled well in advance, which makes it a scheduling no-brainer for us. We put the event on our youth calendar, plan that we're going to need so much per ticket and the meal we have·beforehand, and it's a stress-free, size-appropriate evening. Plus there's the side benefit of showing support to one of our group's members.

A few rules of thumb: Only go to those places where it doesn't matter if there are three of you or 33 of you (we wish). Advertise well in advance so you have the proper number of drivers, or reserve the church van so the "enough seats" pressure is off. *Do not* cancel just because "nobody's coming." That's a real pitfall for smaller groups that tend to stay smaller if they get the reputation of inconsistency. It sends a horrible message to the four students who were going to come. You, another adult, and four teenagers? That's a great event and can become a real memory-maker. Fun times!

Prepare for some odd leadership

Student leadership in the smaller church setting looks different; larger churches could learn from our example. Instead of making student leadership a hierarchy of officers, give everyone a role in leadership based on strengths and giftedness. Help your teenagers develop as leaders without feeling that other students are higher up on the totem pole.

Something else from Mark Cox, who shared insights back in thought #37: *"Our student ministry has always been known for reaching outsiders. One day, we realized we'd become a safe place for teens who wanted a place just for them. So, we started a student-led cell group strategy that would allow our students to grow as leaders and reach outsiders. I met with a bunch of youth pastors who said it wouldn't work. Volunteers literally told me that I was signing my own resignation. In the first two weeks, five students accepted Christ."* Mark found what worked for his students, and they ran with it. I suspect his group isn't so small anymore.

In the midst of odd elements, keep things safe

I talked about this earlier, but here's a little more. Do you have your child-protection policies in place? Have all your adults undergone background checks—and do you continue that process yearly? Do you make sure that there are appropriate ratios of male and female adult leadership? Are you careful about who drives whom home?

It is so much harder in a smaller church to keep up with this, but *it must be done*. Pedophiles look for smaller organizations like your church where it's easier to pull the wool over people's eyes. They know that laws and policies are not held up to the light as much as they are at bigger places. They're just waiting for you to welcome them in.

Your students are too important. Just do it and never assume you know everyone in your church. At a church where I served, we started our background checks and found a male leader who had been on the sex offender registry for almost 10 years. He was a long-time church member, and I am proud to say the situation was handled with love and grace—but it's proof that you just never know.

Handle the odd planning

With a smaller group, you may fall into the mindset that it's easier to fly by the seat of your pants. It may be true, but it's not usually "best practice" and it's definitely not a good habit to get into just because of your poor planning.

But occasionally, spontaneity works in the smaller group's favor. Kelly Bricker from Grace United Methodist Church in Albion, Pennsylvania, has a quick story of how she took advantage of an appropriate on-the-spot plan change:

"My husband and I are the full-time volunteer youth leaders of our sixth- through 12th-graders. Sometimes we have two kids; sometimes we have seven. All of the ministry's responsibilities are ours, like it or not. Actually, we love it. (Sometimes. Most of the time.)

"Occasionally, when I just have the girls show up for youth group, our meeting consists of hitting the local pumpkin farm, then the mall, and finally Borders with a McCafe thrown in. Kinda like last week. It works for us, especially when one of the girls says it was the best day of her life and the others agree."

Kelly shows here that she knows the students in her group and what it takes to build relationships with them. This is spontaneity at its best and the meaning of blessing in ministry to a smaller group. I'm sure Kelly had a great plan mapped out, but she also knew when to discard the plan.

But for the big things? No matter the size of your group, your families need you to plan at least 12 to 18 months ahead. An example of why this is important: Many companies require employees to put in for their summer vacations by the fall months of the previous year—first come, first serve for the vacation calendar. So if you want the right volunteers to travel with you on next summer's trip, your trip planning has to be done by September 1 of this year, complete with dates, costs, forms, and transportation. And by the way, always recruit leaders first before opening the event up to student registration.

With smaller numbers of teenagers, reaching critical mass is tougher, so the more notice you give student families about an upcoming retreat or lock-in or service project or day apart or white-water rafting, the more students you'll have attend.

All because you planned farther out.

THOUGHT #58

You face some odd dynamics

Be careful to watch for a few group dynamics that can plague a smaller youth group. I saw an example of this at a church I was consulting recently. Is it connection or just cliques?

If you asked the 15 students in this church's youth group how much they loved their youth group, they would tell you that the youth ministry rocks their socks off. Great! But that attitude isn't shared by the other 25 teenagers in this church—teenagers who aren't an accepted part of the group. The inside group became so tightly wound around themselves, they couldn't see how they'd become their own giant, unhealthy clique and no one else could wiggle inside.

Give your students clear teaching and direction on how to reach out and welcome new people. Decide ahead of time that the inside jokes—which can make new people feel left out—are only appropriate at other times. Identify exactly how the group will respond when someone new comes, down to who will show the newcomer around and who will sit where. Give the guest a place of honor on the couch. Have people agree to send a follow-up text or e-mail.

THOUGHT #59

You confront some odd situations

All the books, magazines, and conferences in the world can't forecast the odd situation that will arise in your particular church, group, or families. As soon as I've thought I'd heard it all, something freaky pops up. How to deal with something weird when there's no handbook for it? Prayer and coverage.

Pray for the answer only God can provide to whatever weirdness is happening in your youth ministry. Cover yourself by inviting the pastor or other leaders into the conversation so that you're not left teetering out on the limb alone. Other youth workers are an additional source of objective insight. Either way, cover your heart in God and cover your behind by disclosing what's happening.

Teenagers sometimes create an odd faith

It's become popular today for students to morph and meld their own brand of faith. "Moralistic Therapeutic Deism" is the phrase coined in the 2005 book *Soul Searching*.

I can deal with vague or fuzzy theology within the tenets of Christianity. But I start to squirm and feel out of my comfort zone when the youth group absorbs pieces of other world religions.

In a smaller youth group, I never want to drive anyone away or do anything to put one of my students on the defensive. But that was difficult to avoid when I discovered that one of my group's newer students, a really sweet and wonderful girl, had been sharing with everyone in our group of nine all about how she and her parents were pagan Wiccans. She had been telling some of the girls the more inner details at one of our overnight events. No one else seemed troubled by it—just me.

I've been doing this youth ministry thing for a long time and times like these still keep me on my toes. What do I do? I pray without ceasing for every sentence in my chats with that questioning teenager. Walking softly and carefully is also required instead of a "bull in the spiritual china shop" approach.

First and foremost, I show loving acceptance but never apologize for the "hope that I have in Christ Jesus." I don't change anything we're going to study; what we study will always make a beeline back to Jesus. But I also don't put teenagers in an uncomfortable public spot about their faith. I place a huge amount of faith into the work of the Holy Spirit to whisper into the hearts of my students, especially when they're seeking answers on the reality of the one true God. The student with a mushy faith will learn volumes by what you and I do, as long as it doesn't contradict what we say.

navigating your church's channels

THOUGHT #61 Who's the captain?

This book is being read by a wide variety of youth workers: full-time paid, part-time paid, part-time unpaid, full-time unpaid, part of the volunteer team, maybe even a senior pastor or two.

Whatever place you hold in your church's organizational chart, you serve on the youth ministry deck of the Good Ship (insert your church's name here). The first thing you should find out (and then give your loyalty to) is who's the captain of the ship. Yes, Jesus is the captain of our souls, but who's heading up your church? Who's in charge of the ministry work you're doing? It's not always clear in every ministry situation, which leads to indefinable markers of success and unrealized expectations. Heartache and pain often follow in the wake.

Make sure you know the proper channels for your ministry involvement. Ask questions like, "Who do I report to? What is the chain of command?" Once you have that clearly charted out, follow and honor that leadership. If you can't? Get off the ship.

THOUGHT #62

Where's the ship's log?

I used to say, "Leave a wide paper trail" of your activities in youth ministry. I'm still a huge proponent of that—just make it an electronic paper trail.

Here's what I mean and why: Most youth workers who find themselves in trouble, sometimes big trouble, never saw it coming. I know I didn't at the Church-That-Shall-Not-Be-Named. But I was in deep waters before the sun went down and the pumpkin patch had closed. The phone wires were already buzzing to the senior pastor's vacation home. All because I didn't communicate what should be done with some rotten pumpkins and the teenagers' pickup time.

OK, so here are ways to avoid a similar nightmare experience:

- Include your supervising pastor or leader on every e-mail, like keeping a captain's log. Follow up any phone calls to other leaders or parents with an e-mail saying, "Here's what I heard in our convo. Is that how you heard it?"
- Send or e-mail notes home with details of everything.

- Post what's happening in the church newsletter, bulletin, on the bulletin board, on the church website and youth page, on Facebook®, by mass text, in smoke signals, on a message in a bottle—whatever it takes to make sure everyone's on the same page.
- Stick to what you said you were going to do.

Communicate, communicate, communicate. This is a key to keeping you out of trouble and your ministry navigating forward.

THOUGHT #63

Who's the first mate?

In a smaller church, guess who the first mate is? The next in command after the pastor, the one who makes the real decisions and has major influence within the church. The one who holds the key to joy or heartache for your day. That's right—it's probably the church secretary!

Want to be smart? Keep the secretary on your good side. Never treat the admin people like they work for you; serve them as if you work for them. Give them what they need, and obey their deadlines. There's a reason they've set dates in place; honoring those dates helps you and your ministry in the long run. Keep the office informed of your schedule and plans. Most importantly, be obedient to the church calendar and make sure your youth dates get on as quickly as possible. After all, the church van is usually first come, first served.

Oh and *never, ever* forget the church secretary's birthday. You only make that mistake once.

#64   **The rest of the crew**

In a small church, most staff people are stretched as thin as you are. Keeping that in mind will go a long way toward keeping you out of shark-filled waters. I bet you rushed home, fed the kids and yourself, buckled everyone into the car, and raced to church—but your last-minute needs do not constitute another staff person's emergency. Again, the key to avoiding upsetting the other staff and keeping smooth waters? Be organized before the last minute arrives. Yes, I mean you!

#65   **Swab the deck!**

Boost the reputation of your church's youth ministry by making sure you and your ministry clean up after every facility usage. Smaller churches have little to no custodial help. Teach your students good stewardship, make them clean up, and you'll find they make less mess. If your teenagers used it, moved it, drank from it, ate off of it, threw it, tossed it, brewed it, mixed it, drove it, or played with it, make sure it's returned to its former state once you're done.

THOUGHT

#66

Don't even get on board

Some of us enter our church's youth ministry because we've been attending our church for a while. Others are hired from the outside. If you're the latter, thoroughly check out a church's youth ministry DNA before getting on board.

Andrew Suite is a youth pastor from Florida who knows a thing or two about church staffing change: *"Try to discern church tension or unrest. One church I served had a history of short tenure youth directors. Couple this with a split over a move to a new building, followed by hurricane damage to the new facility and you have a church with an amazing story of faith—but an anxious spirit. A healthy and holy discontent with regards to the status quo and advancing the kingdom is good, but anxiousness and unrest run counter to the gospel of peace."*

It turned out that Andrew became one more youth worker in a long line of collateral damage. The key is to not get on staff in the first place at a church that eats up its youth workers and spits them out every few years.

So Andrew's search for a new church position began, and here's a bullet he dodged: *"One church offered me a position less than a week after my first online interview with them. I hadn't even met anyone in person and had to ask them to slow down a bit and let me visit first. Perhaps I was a bit hasty in accepting, but several factors caused them to rescind their offer. In retrospect, I'm glad we didn't move only to find out later they weren't solid on what they were looking for in the position."*

THOUGHT
#67

When it's time to jump ship

Sensing the wind has changed direction at your church? Wondering if it's time for you to move on? I'm not advocating abandoning ship unless you sense that God is calling you elsewhere and using the church's circumstances to do so. But if you've begun to wonder whether it's time to stay or go, here are a few questions to ask yourself:

- Am I at peace serving this church?
- Do I often go home with a headache, tears, or huge amounts of stress?
- Do I dread going to work?
- Am I hearing God's still, small voice leading me somewhere else?

These are sure signs it may be time to pray about whether God is calling you to serve elsewhere. Begin to sharpen up your resume just in case.

THOUGHT #68

The ship sailed without you

Are you about to be or have you been fired? Asked to resign? Don't be ashamed; it's happened to many of us.

Leave well and with integrity. Please don't do the passive-aggressive thing where you play people against each other. If you hear yourself saying any of the following three sentences, tape up your mouth with duct tape and walk away:

1) *"The church/pastor/leaders/parents/board is forcing me out!"* It doesn't matter who made the call. What matters is that it's happening and it's time to go.

2) *"They'll never be able to replace me."* Yes they will. The only ministry staff person who was ever irreplaceable was Jesus, and even he sent someone else to finish the work.

3) *"Everyone's on my side."* If you think you're going to win some courtroom scene where you get to

debate the issue at hand, you're wrong. And by the way, Senior Pastor always trumps Youth Pastor. That's one you won't win.

Friend, if things in your ministry have come to the point of anything like I've described above, do the kingdom a favor and quietly move on. How you leave will follow you in good or bad ways. Don't leave a trail of broken teenagers in the dirt as you leave.

THOUGHT #69   Chart your course

In other words, map out where your ministry is going and require a full, comprehensive job description. Chances are you will have to draft the job description yourself, but it's important. Make sure the description includes the reality of hours spent on the ministry, including those at home. This allows everyone in church leadership to have a clear snapshot of the job and to work off the same page.

Without a clear direction for where you and the ministry are headed, the rest of the people in your church will just fill in their own mental blanks of what they think you should be accomplishing. The end result is that it leads everyone down different tributaries, sending the ministry off course. Then it gets stuck and mired in shallow discussion on what you should or shouldn't be doing. Endless conversations ensue on how many teenagers should be coming, where the next mission trip should be, or how much to charge for dinner on Sunday nights.

All of this can be avoided by making sure there's a roadmap guiding your ministry's twists and turns. Not what you alone or a few leaders think, but a conglomeration of everyone's thoughts on the youth ministry's values, mission, target, goals, benchmarks, and other priorities.

THOUGHT #70

Smooth sailing

Does this describe your ministry life? You love being a youth worker. Things are appropriately balanced and happy at home. Your relationship with God is sweet and peaceful. The youth at your church are growing closer to each other and to their Creator. Your church's leadership is happy with your service, and you're happy with their investment into your ministry. All is well with your soul.

Praise God from whom all blessings flow!

Praise Him all creatures here below!

Praise Him above ye Heavenly Host!

Praise Father, Son and Holy Ghost! Amen!

doing more ministry with less money

Your budget will never be big enough

From Mark Cox (he's an honest guy, with the voice for a lot of his cohort):

"For those of us that didn't get into youth ministry to crunch numbers and balance a budget—which is most of us—we need help planning. I'm so used to going by the seat of my pants, I usually end up halfway through the year with most of my budget being gone. For those of us that want to be responsible, we need help!"

Mark, this chapter is for you! For the rest of you, unless you have some wealthy anonymous benefactor, your ministry is probably under-budgeted. Raise your hand if you have thousands of dollars left over at the end of your youth ministry budget year. Yeah, I didn't think so.

Turn to businesses or corporations

Joel Snyder from Richfield, Pennsylvania, had this to say: *"Our church doesn't allow fundraisers, so we use a business (Cruiser's Cafe) to help us. For example, this month each Tuesday 20 percent of our proceeds go to our OCC mission trip. It is a win for our ministry and a win for our business!"*

Check with your local merchants and big businesses. Companies like Chick-fil-A®, Olive Garden®, and Wal-Mart® have supply donation policies and budgets to put money back into their local communities. I've had luck in the past with Christian-based insurance companies that matched my group's fundraising dollar for dollar. Many restaurants will set up "church night" at their establishment. Hey, we all have to eat!

Put the "fun" back in fundraising

I find nothing "fun" about fundraising. It's a sticky subject in so many churches. Should the youth ministry raise funds? Do fundraising events take away from the church's overall giving levels? And if the students do fundraisers, what's the best way to keep track: an even division of funds among all youth or an hourly rate so teenagers get paid for how much they worked? Can parents work in their place? What kinds of fundraisers work best? Should you sell or not sell stuff? The mental stroll down my personal fundraiser memory lane gives me a headache!

I asked my Facebook® friends to share their tips for making their youth ministry dollar stretch. Travis Williams, a youth guy from North Canton, Ohio, posted this: *"Instead of bombarding our members with endless small fundraisers that bring in only a few bucks (car washes, bake sales... but only net us $200 to $400), we researched a bigger fundraiser. We are currently doing a pumpkin patch through a company specializing in church fundraising, and it is amazing! My students work in the evenings; parents watch it during the day. It takes organization and time but is so much more effective than small fundraisers. It leaves us with more time for other things."* Others echoed that sentiment with similar ideas, such as a golf tournament, refreshments during a sports season, and massive church yard sales where table space was rented.

THOUGHT #74   Let parents help

Tom Pounder, a youth ministry blogger at ministryblackboard.com, shared this thought about working with a small budget: *"A limited budget can be very challenging, which is why you have to be creative in how you spend your money. One way we've saved money* is by getting parents involved. We organize a needs list and send it out to the parents and adults in our church. Parents usually respond in full force! They're eager to help, especially when they know it's for something their children will benefit from."

My young buddy Tyler Smither, at Maples Memorial United Methodist Church in Olive Branch, Mississippi, puts it like I feel it: *"I hate fundraisers with an undying passion. However, they are necessary. I found there are few things parents love more than seeing their kids do fundraisers. Why? No idea. Maybe it is that 'it keeps my teenager from being lazy' mentality. Either way, if you combine my loathing of fundraisers and the parents' love affair for them, you get one thing. Parents lead the fundraisers, which is perfect for me. The ministry gets the cash, and I don't get the headache."*

THOUGHT #75 Share your resources

Otherwise known as "share your stuff." How to do that? Develop a youth ministry inventory sheet, make copies and take the idea to your local youth workers' network. Get everyone to fill out what books, games, props, and other resources each ministry has available. Put the info on a spreadsheet and send a copy to everyone. Let the borrowing commence! A side benefit will be developing stronger friendship connections with the youth workers around you. From Mark Cox: *"This is why I love youth ministry conferences so much! I think that there are a lot of us who benefit from other youth pastors. One conversation with a local youth pastor can help you solve some of your biggest problems! For instance, I met with a local youth pastor to talk about a combo event we were working on. Not only did we end up talking about sharing resources, each of us had answers to the other's questions. We left not only with solutions but also with a relationship which is still strong today."*

THOUGHT #76

Look for the deep pockets

So we're all usually scrambling to fill in the financial blanks, right? I know you know this, but some of you may be forgetting to take advantage of a simple truth: Find your deep pockets—and I don't mean in your baggy pants. Find the adults in your church who may not be able to volunteer time but would love to contribute by getting or giving the ministry anything it really needs. These people are out there!

Over the years, I've discovered adults who possessed the spiritual gift of giving. Among the *many* blessings my ministry received: $1,500 every Christmas for 10 students to go on winter retreat; a mom who purchased all of our weekly meal food, as long as she didn't have to cook it;

parents who refurnished our youth room with really cool new furniture; adults who paid for other adults to attend conferences; and so on.

Remember, you must look for these people—or find the person who finds these people. Many parents won't think of the idea first but just have to be asked. Instead of simply handing over a check to a bottomless pit, they want to feel like they're helping in a specific area. It feels more purposeful to them, which tends to make it a repeated action. Yay!

From Ben Halsch: *"Make sure to constantly cast your youth vision to adults. Having them on board can help so much. You can even go to them to purchase things in your ministry, especially if you have a very small or no budget. Having those good relationships makes asking for money a lot easier."*

You said it, Ben. Asking for financial help is a lot easier if church members know and believe in what the ministry is striving to accomplish.

THOUGHT #77

How to figure your budget

Wonder what figure to use in determining a healthy budget? In his book *Sustainable Youth Ministry*, Mark DeVries, president of Youth Ministry Architects, said that a good rule of thumb is $1,000 to $1,500 annually per teenager, including your program budget and salaries. Without proper funding based on the number of students you want to reach, your youth ministry probably will stay right where it is. When underfunded, a repeating cycle of short-term staff people flows in and out. The program itself seems to start and stop, to flame up and then flutter out.

THOUGHT #78

What to do with your budget

Here's a back-and-forth Facebook® conversation between two of my youth ministry friends, Lawrence Powers and John Mulholland, about their budgets:

Lawrence: *"First I make sure I turn in a budget request that is THOROUGH so 'they' have no question on what I need and why. I also put the money into the 'more important' line items first and then work my way down. We do fundraisers to help offset the costs but also don't charge full price for our students. Our chaperones never pay. Still, it's a stretch."*

John: *"I like the thorough budget request. I did that last year, and everyone knew exactly what I was asking for."*

Lawrence: *"It helps because if they don't want to give you what you asked for, they can tell you what they think you should cut."*

I like Lawrence's suggestion of asking finance committee members to help you determine what's not valuable and can be cut from your budget. It places a sense of ownership on their shoulders, and they can't blindly make rash decisions.

THOUGHT #79

Keep your finance committee people informed

Phil Bell is in youth ministry at Community Bible Church in Brighton, Michigan. Read what he had to say: *"We have the students bring $1 to cover food costs. As simple as it sounds, it's made a huge difference by cutting costs. It also created a step of student ownership, moving them away from a consumer mentality, and built bridges with the 'budget people.' If the finance committee sees that students are owning the solution, it will give them a favorable viewpoint when working on the next budget."*

Phil reminded me that we do have to report to others about our financial responsibility for youth ministry finances. If this is an area of weakness for you, *please* do yourself a huge favor and turn it over to someone. Don't get yourself in trouble for poor reporting practices. Find someone who is a computer geek and excels in Excel spreadsheets. Lack of good recordkeeping has placed many youth workers' jobs in jeopardy and can damage a ministry's reputation.

THOUGHT #80

Set a standard with your tithe

Have you thought about teaching tithing to your students by tithing on the gifts given to your ministry? Or on the money earned in fundraisers? Involve the whole group in researching what God's Word has to say. If you do decide to tithe as a group on the monies earned, the hands-on learning from deciding together where to tithe will make a powerful impact on your students for their own offerings to God.

a few of my favorite things

These next 15 thoughts are broken up into three "five favorite" themes of doing youth ministry and being better at what you do; they've worked for me. None of them are earth shattering; just my current personal favorites. You can write your five favs in your book.

Five Programming Ideas

Prayer Breakfast Club

This idea may not be new, but I saw it in a new light recently when consulting with a church in Oxford, Mississippi, about its youth ministry. It's the simplest thing to pull off, yet all the students seemed to *love* it. Scored huge in their ministry asset area.

It's as simple as this: Find a local breakfast place where the setting works and the food is grab and go. Schedule your students to come every week at 7 a.m. or whatever time works for your schools. Parents drop teenagers off, the students order their food, and everyone sits together in a designated area. You have a brief devotional ready—either verbal or in written form—take prayer requests, pray, and then take students to school in the church van or with other arranged drivers.

So simple! The students at the Mississippi church called it a "must do" for every week and brought friends, too. It got so big—even though their group was small—that they divided up the club, middle school on one day and senior high another. Yes, it's early in the day but it had big impact with high visibility and low maintenance.

THOUGHT #82

Suitcase Safari

This is not a new idea and I've heard it called by other things, but I like this twist on it. With a name like Suitcase Safari, the only hint I would give the students is a list of weird items to bring and then find interesting ways to work that weirdness into the weekend. I also like how Tyler Smither at Maples Memorial United Methodist Church in Olive Branch, Mississippi, does it in the fall and not in the summer.

"Suitcase Safari is a trip I like to do in the fall where basically the kids have no idea where they are going until we get there. All they know is we're going somewhere. The mystery aspect really adds to the trip, and for the few weeks prior,

students constantly ask me where we were going. There is an excitement already built into the trip. What I find kinda cool is how excited the parents get about it. We let them know where we're going but swear them to secrecy. They have a great time withholding this precious info from their kids. When parents are excited and buy into it, the students do, too. Case in point: I was expecting 15-18 students to sign up and ended up taking 27. It sells itself. I love Suitcase Safari!"

THOUGHT #83

Local outreach efforts

Some of your best outreach efforts can happen in your own backyard. Identify needs in your community, partner with other churches or local organizations, recruit volunteers and resources from your congregation, and unleash your students to make a difference! Here are some reasons these efforts work well:

1) Community service projects allow teenagers who've never done a mission week a chance to grow their serving skills.

2) Staying local means your immediate impact stays local. Mission trips to other nations are incredible experiences, but imagine how your students' lives will be changed as they see frequent reminders of their outreach efforts!

3) If you partner with other churches or organizations, you reduce your expenses and make the outreach much more affordable for your students and their families.

Other outreach efforts

While I'm a big fan of local outreach efforts, I also know the rewards of taking students on mission trips to other cities, states, and nations. If you team up with the right organization, they'll often do all the prep work: the programming, spiritual emphasis, meal, project planning. What do you do? Show up with your teenagers. The cost can be reasonable, and the experience gives your students a taste of the exciting serving opportunities they might experience in other mission settings.

Many organizations offer these kinds of opportunities, and if you've never done an international mission trip, you might not want to start there. Instead, choose a ministry planning an outreach in another part of your state, a building project in a rural region, or some other worthwhile effort. These experiences can be great building blocks for the overseas trip you may someday choose to pursue.

Rites of passage

Rites of passage—those significant moments of transition in your students' lives—are *so* much easier to do in a smaller group, and you can do them really well. Rites of passage include celebrating a fifth- or sixth-grader's rise into the middle school youth, confirmation, welcoming in new freshmen, or a big sendoff for your graduates.

In a smaller setting, you can bring the entire church into sharing and affirming each student in personal ways. Teenagers gain strength and powerful memories as a congregation displays love and Christ-like support in these moments. Church members often know those graduates and have watched them grow up; they want to be on the inside of the party!

Plan the party, buy the cake, purchase gifts of Bibles and let others inscribe in them, share in praying over each student, collect personalized cards for each teenager, and invite everyone! Make it a church family event—because it is.

Five Affirmation Ideas

THOUGHT #86

Birthdays!

Students' birthdays remain a "must do" with me. This is Youth Pastor 101. Don't try telling me you're really bad at remembering birthdays or always think about sending the card *after* you see it on Facebook® or no teenager really cares about you remembering. Bad excuses.

We celebrate birthdays because they're a chance to focus on the one instead of the many. It's a chance for you to say and for the teenager to hear: "Hey, I value you! I'm glad you were born and I pray you have a wonderful day. You deserve it!" Who isn't blessed for hearing that?

I'll let you off the hook a little. If you really are bad about remembering birthdays, then find someone who isn't. Recruit a student or adult volunteer who is great at sending out cards. Facebook® has made it so easy; post on students' walls. I know how excited I got about my posts my last birthday!

THOUGHT #87

To see and be seen

Attend students' events—games, plays, concerts. They love seeing you there. If it can't be you, make sure someone from your leadership team goes. Make sure they see you there. Follow the event up with a quick text or Facebook® post. Use technology to engage in their world. It's still all about relationships and meeting teenagers in their world, not yours.

THOUGHT #88 Postcards from the edge

Postcards are fun to get. Who doesn't like getting snail mail—especially when it's not junk mail or a bill or something else boring? When you travel someplace without your students, send them postcards.

Here are my secrets (and if you tell my students, I will hunt you down): I often purchase the cards ahead of time and start on them before I ever leave. Or I buy them at the airport right after I get off the plane. I carry postcard stamps and a set of mailing labels and get the cards mailed first thing from my city of destination. What can I say? I like to be efficient and it's the thought that counts, right? If my students want to picture me hunched over my hotel room desk at 2:30 a.m. writing out cards, who am I to judge?

THOUGHT #89 Look 'em in the eyes

Eye-to-eye conversations are really the most affirming thing you can do. Studies show that teenagers spend, on average, less than two minutes a week in direct eye-to-eye conversation and that's with their parents!

Take the time at each youth group event to talk directly *with* each student and not *at* each student. Sit down with students and look them in the face. It doesn't have to be a deep connection—just real conversation.

Scripture verses

Sharing a specific Scripture with a student can have more impact than you know. When a Bible verse hits you for a particular student, let that person know. Send a text, post a comment on Facebook®, write a note—do something. Just speak that word from the Word into the teenager's life. About eight or nine years ago, I caught up with a former student who opened his Bible to show me a verse I'd written down for him several years before that. He's a full-time missionary today.

Five Resources to Make You a Better Youth Worker

Pack your bags!

Go to a youth ministry training conference. Seriously. Find the money, get people to sponsor you, sell your doghouse, cut out Starbucks®, get a roomie, find people to carpool with—whatever it takes to get you there.

You'll come away with your head about to explode from all the ideas. That's good! You'll have laughed, cried, worshiped, played, eaten, slept (who am I kidding?), learned, grown, networked, and deepened.

Subscribe to magazines

Every youth worker should read at least one youth ministry magazine. You'll find all kinds of ideas and inspiration and insights that will help you grow as a leader and a follower of Christ. By the way, my personal fav is GROUP Magazine— and once you find your favorite youth ministry magazine, consider getting the bulk rate so you can bless and train your volunteers.

If there's only time for one book…

Sustainable Youth Ministry by Mark DeVries (published by InterVarsity Press) is a true blueprint for creating stronger, forward-moving youth ministries. Mark's book is funny, insightful, practical, and doable for even the smaller size ministry. It's a must-read for youth workers.

Leadership Manual 101

The Bible: Who would have thunk it? In addition to being the book from which we can gather our daily bread, it's full of great leadership principles. Examples include Moses' need to not be Super Leader, Jesus' leadership organizational chart, how to recognize and utilize each person's giftedness, and what to do and not do from the example of guys like Timothy and Peter.

Coffee, coffee, and more...

Coffee. I love it. Massive amounts of caffeine will make you a better youth worker. Drink it day and night like I do. See how I turned out? No wait, bad example if you've met me. I just always wanted to read about the importance of coffee in a book. I can die a happy youth pastor now.

four things i wish someone told me earlier

#96   Get over yourself

I wish someone had told me how full of myself I was in my younger years of youth ministry. I bragged about what I knew about students, but the reality was, I didn't have teenagers of my own. Who was I to tell parents what to do?

And oh, the way I mentioned my youth ministry numbers during conversation or how I'd talk about the A-listers I knew in the youth ministry world. I can hardly stand it when I think about it. I worked too hard at having to prove myself and my worth in the youth ministry world.

Be who you are, and value where you are in the youth ministry scheme of things. It's OK to say "I'm young" or "I'm old." We all have something to bring to students and youth ministry. At every stage of the journey, if God has us there, then he will use us in the way he knows is best. Now that's value!

Repeat after me, "I'm sorry about that"

A defensive attitude is a ministry and career killer. No one really wants to hear your excuses or a passive-aggressive attempt at blaming someone else for what went wrong. What about when a parent is in your face and it's truly not your fault? Just say, "I'm sorry about that," "I'm sorry that happened," "I'll make sure I do better next time," "I'll take care of it personally," or "Thank you for bringing it to my attention."

THOUGHT #98

Keep your friends close—and your enemies far away

Surround yourselves with people you love working with and who love working with you. You won't win your nemesis over, so don't think you will by putting them in a crucial leadership place. They don't like you and you can't change that, so move on.

Time and truth go hand-in-hand

Youth ministry is a series of spiritual and emotional ups and downs. Sometimes the rollercoaster ride from "You're the best youth worker ever" to "Why did they hire this person?" is so fast, you get whiplash. It can all turn in a moment.

One thing I know to be true. "Time and truth go hand-in-hand." I don't even know who first said this, but I know who shared it with me. My friend, Wolfy, an older volunteer at one of my churches. He was consoling me after I was confronted about saying something I didn't say. He said, "Stephanie, God works it all together for his good. You're called to his purpose to serve these young people. Give it enough time and the truth will come out. It always does."

Wise words, Wolfy.